Sports

Hockey

by Nick Rebman

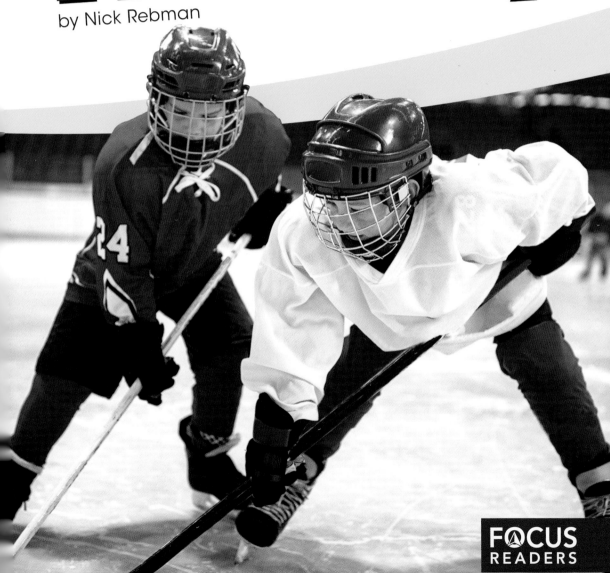

FOCUS
READERS

www.focusreaders.com

Focus Readers is distributed by North Star Editions:
sales@northstareditions.com | 888-417-0195

Produced for Focus Readers by Red Line Editorial.

Photographs ©: Lucky Business/Shutterstock Images, cover, 1, 13; Sergei Butorin/ Shutterstock Images, 4, 11, 16 (bottom left); Lorraine Swanson/Shutterstock Images, 7, 16 (top left); ArtBoyMB/iStockphoto, 9; DardaInna/Shutterstock Images, 15; Julia Sudnitskaya/Shutterstock Images, 16 (top right); Ievgen Z/Shutterstock Images, 16 (bottom right)

ISBN
978-1-63517-920-0 (hardcover)
978-1-64185-022-3 (paperback)
978-1-64185-224-1 (ebook pdf)
978-1-64185-123-7 (hosted ebook)

Library of Congress Control Number: 2018931986

Printed in the United States of America
Mankato, MN
May, 2018

About the Author

Nick Rebman enjoys reading, drawing, and traveling to places where he doesn't speak the language. He lives in Minnesota.

Table of Contents

Hockey

Hockey is fun.

Two teams play.

They play on ice.

A player needs a **puck**.

A player needs a stick.

A player needs **skates**.

stick

skate

puck

Safety

Players stay safe.

They have **pads**.

They have **helmets**.

helmet

pad

9

How to Play

Players skate on the ice.

They pass the puck.

They use their sticks.

A player shoots the puck.

The puck goes into the net.

This is called a goal.

net

One team scores
more goals.
This team wins.
The players are
happy.

Glossary

helmets

puck

pads

skates

Index